Pineapple

A play

Robert Messik

Samuel French — London
www.samuelfrench-london.co.uk

FOR AMATEUR PRODUCTION ENQUIRIES

UNITED KINGDOM AND WORLD
EXCLUDING NORTH AMERICA
plays@samuelfrench.co.uk
020 7255 4302/01

Each title is subject to availability from Samuel French, depending upon country of performance.

PINEAPPLE

First presented on 26 August 2006 by Drip Action Theatre Company at 55 Tarrant Street as part of the Arundel Festival with the following company:

Peter   Kate Smith
Jill   Simon Weston

Directed by John Griffiths
Stage managed by Tonya James

CHARACTERS

Peter, 41
Jill, 32

Time—the present

For Kelly

PINEAPPLE

The set should look as much like the living-room of a flat in north-west London as it possibly can

There is a front door, a door to the bedroom and a door to the kitchen. The living-room is designed by Ikea. Everything: a sofa, coffee table, units, a sideboard with a drawer and a pouffe with storage space inside, right down to the pictures on the wall, are from the Swedish superstore. There is a bottle of whisky and some glasses on the sideboard. In one of its drawers is an "A - Z". In the pouffe is a video manual. Photos on the units show a couple, Peter and Jill, in various locations round Britain. There are also several clocks around the room, a television with video, a thermostat, a telephone and an intercom. Two suitcases sit by the front door. The living-room is extremely tidy

Noises come from behind the front door

Peter (*off*) So that's ... mm hmm ...will you ... no ... just read tha —— read that ... if you could just read that back ... thank yo —— yes ... yes ... yes ... with cheese ... yes ... yes ... no. No. No ... no, no, no, no ... yes ...

Keys are heard in the lock of the front door and Peter, 41, lets himself in, whilst talking on his mobile. He wears an old suit and carries a briefcase and three bottles of wine, two white and one red. He puts them down on the sideboard

...That's it ... Good. Marvellous ... Let me give you my —— hello?

Peter has been put on hold. He hums "Babushka" by Kate Bush

... Of course, you're busy, fine ... my address. My address yes. It's Flat ten, seventy-five ... Flat ten ... ten ... as in one, two, three, four, five, six, seven, eight, nine, ten, eleven. Ten. That's it. Seventy-five Wrenview ... Like Sir Christopher Wre —— St Paul's? ... W.R.E.N ... yes. View as in ... V.I.E.W. Great. Thank yo —— Whoah, whoah, whoah, whoah, whoah, you're still doing the half-hour rule?

A toilet flushes from the bathroom off the bedroom

Not delivered in half an hour pizza comes for ... yes ... for free, yes ... twenty-five minutes? ... Confident. What time you have? ... Exactly? ... Exac —— Great. Ready, set, go.

Without taking his eyes off his watch, Peter hangs up the phone. He speeds round the room, checking all the other clocks are set to the right time. He moves to the sideboard, picks up the clock and tries to work the mechanism

As he's running around doing all this, Peter's wife, Jill, 32, comes out of the bedroom. She wears an outdoor coat and carries a handbag and is in the final stages of pregnancy. She stares

Jill You're here. Home. Here, home early ——
Peter Every second counts ——
Jill Half an hour early ——
Peter How small do they expect your fingers to be?
Jill You're never home at this time.
Peter Knife? (*He stares at Jill*)

Jill stares back

Peter vanishes into the kitchen

Jill doesn't move from her spot

Peter emerges from the kitchen with a knife

Every second. It's happened in the past. (*He uses the knife to open the back of the clock. He adjusts the time*) I have one time, the takeaway's got another. No surprises which they go with. Done. Only real way to do it, of course. People could make up all the times they want. You're late. I want my free pizza. Place would be out of business in a week. Video manual?

Jill Sorry?

Peter Manual, manual. Video manual.

Jill In the ——

Peter
Jill } (*together*) Pouffe ...

Peter fishes out the manual and then lies in front of the video

Jill takes a deep breath

Jill Peter ... (*No words come out*)

Peter I would like to meet the person that fully claims to understand these things.

Jill tries again; she takes a deep breath

Jill Peter, I'm ... (*She can't say any more*)

Peter I'd shake him by the hand; buy him a drink.

Jill's getting really frustrated

Jill I don't want to do this any more ...

Peter Because these are nothing short of a mys —— got it. (*He finishes with the video and stands back up*) Now we wait. Jam-packed on the A1. Lights are out, burst water main or something. They'll never get through. Not even on one of those ... those little bike things.

Jill Scooter.

Peter Those little bike things. Make a sound like a giant wasp.

Jill Scooter.

Peter Government should ban them. Can never remember the name.

Jill screams

Jill SCOOTER.

A silence. Peter points to the wine

Peter Thought we'd make an evening of it. There was an offer. Three for the price of two. Thought why not. Why not? You could have one glass. One glass wouldn't hurt. You should sit down. Better for the —— (*He walks towards Jill*)
Jill No.

Peter goes back to the wine

Peter Two white, one red. Wasn't sure which way round to do it, but that felt like a compromise.

Peter looks at Jill in her outdoor coat

Not taking your coat off?

Peter goes into the bedroom

Jill, who hasn't yet moved, takes out a letter and stares at it

(*Off*) You'll never guess who I saw today. Whatshername? The one with the lazy eye. Had some laser operation to cure her sight, scratched the retina, now stares at everything really intently. Off-putting if you're not prepared.
Jill You didn't ——
Peter (*off*) We didn't chat. Of course not. You remember the name? Haven't seen her in ——
Jill Two and a half years.
Peter (*off*) Two and a half years. Not since ... Driving me mad. Sally? Sally something? Is it Sally? Sally ——
Jill Karen. Golding.

Peter (*off*) Yes. Thank you. Saw her today. Across the street.

Peter comes back out of the bedroom. He's changed into more casual clothes

Chilly? (*He pats her stomach*) Incubating nicely. I'll put the heating on.

Jill I'm fine.

Peter No trouble. Warm the place a bit. Been a mild month, so the money's there.

Jill OK.

Peter turns the thermostat up, listening intently for the click to signify the heating's working

Peter Best money we spent, that. Don't mind holding my hands up to say I was wrong and you, right, right, right. Glad I listened.

Peter squeezes Jill's arm. She doesn't react

Be warmer in a minute. Take your coat off then.

Peter waits for Jill to take her coat off. She doesn't move

I'll get you a cardy.

Peter goes back into the bedroom

Sounds can be heard of Peter going through the wardrobe. Jill waits for the inevitable

(*Off*) Best time of the year this, nip in the air, but then we get home and are safe and ...

A pause. Peter comes back out of the bedroom

Been doing some clearing out, eh? Cupboard seems a bit bare. Hope you haven't overdone it.

Jill says nothing

Good idea though. Bit of a spring clean. Even though it's October. Just a saying after all.

A silence

Jill Peter ——
Peter Where do you think it comes from? The saying? Spring cleaning? Probably the Christians. Maybe cleaning out all the pagans.
Jill Peter, please ——
Peter Ever stopped to think where we'd be if things had gone differently? Pagans on top? Be heading home from a hard day's sacrificing. Or maybe a mass orgy.
Jill Stop talking for just one moment. Please.
Peter I always talk, you know that. As long as I keep talking seems I've got a handle on the ——
Jill Shut up ——
Peter — status quo.

A pause

Heating's come on.
Jill Oh God.
Peter Just saying.
Jill You're making this so much harder than it needed to be.
Peter Sorry.
Jill Stop it.
Peter What am I ——
Jill Stop ——
Peter I don't know what ——
Jill Stop it, stop it, stop it, just stop it.

A pause. Peter is about to say something

Stop. It. Don't say anything. OK? Not a word. Nothing. Nothing. Christ, it wasn't meant to happen like thi —— Stop ... I was going to slip away, quietly, easily, without a fuss. You were going to come home, on time, find the note ... Oh, Christ. Oh good Christ Almight ——

Jill starts hyperventilating. Peter gets a brown paper bag from her handbag. He hands it to her. She takes it and starts breathing into it

Peter You want some water?
Jill I'm ... (*she takes a breath*) ... leave ... (*breath*) ... ing ... (*breath*) ... you.
Peter Maybe a cup of tea?
Jill Stop being so ... (*breath*) ... fuck ... (*breath*) ... ing, Peter.

Peter guides her to the sofa

Peter Water. And I'll put the kettle on. You want to be taking it easy.

Jill throws the bag down in frustration

Jill For fuck's ——

Peter shoves Jill's head between her legs, as far as the bump will allow

Peter goes into the kitchen and pours a glass of water. He turns the kettle on. He comes back holding a glass of water

Peter Here.

Jill, her head still between her legs, reaches out and takes the water. She drinks. She hands the glass back to Peter. A pause

Better? (*He sits*)

Jill Bit.
Peter Good-o.

A pause

Jill Any biscuits in there?
Peter Pizza'll be here soon. Free pizza.
Jill I'm not staying.
Peter No.

A beat

Just there's a lot coming. I ordered the banquet.
Jill I'm not staying.
Peter I see that. Just a shame to waste it.

A pause

Jill I'll get my own biscuit.
Peter No, no.

*Peter gets up and goes into the kitchen. A moment later, he emerges
with two different biscuits, a Bourbon and a digestive*

Didn't know which one you wanted. Digestive's better with tea.
Bourbon stands on its own.

*Jill considers which biscuit to take, then goes for both. She eats the
Bourbon quickly. Peter looks at her stomach*

Peter Eating for ——
Jill Don't.

A silence. Jill munches on the digestive

Aren't you going to say anything?

Peter You'll ruin your appetite.
Jill Not about the bloody pizza.
Peter Just pointing out.
Jill About our impending divorce?
Peter Might just be a separation.
Jill It's not.
Peter Might be.
Jill It's not.

A pause

Peter If I'd have known, I wouldn't have ordered the banquet.

Jill slaps Peter, hard across the face. A pause

Jill You're in shock. By giving you another shock. Cancels first shock out.

Peter considers this. He picks up the phone and presses speed dial. Jill watches in disbelief

Peter Why don't you sort out that tea? Kettle's just boil —— (*Into the phone*) Hello? Hi ... no, I don't mind holding. (*To Jill*) Longer I hold, later the pizza. (*He waits. He sings, "Wuthering Heights" by Kate Bush*)

Jill looks as if she might consider saying something, but instead goes to make the tea

... Not a problem. Name's Mr Wilson, I ordered a pizza about nine and a half minutes ago, coming to seventy-five Wrenview ... as in Sir Christopher Wre —— St. Paul's? ... W.R.E.N ... yes. View as in ... V.I.E.W ... Just wanted to check on its progress. Thanks. (*He resumes "Wuthering Heights"*) ... Hi. ... Just leaving now? Super.

Jill comes back out of the kitchen with two cups of tea. She puts them on the table, not caring that the tea spills

Jill Tea.
Peter Great news.
Jill You've thought about what I said?
Peter They're only just leaving. Never in a million years going to get to us in twenty ... (*He looks at his watch*) ... one minutes. Never going to happen. We're going to get a free dinner. Not counting the wine of course, but then that's almost a luxury and three for the price of two, the economics speak for themselves.

Jill smashes a cup. A silence. Peter stares at the spreading stain

Jill You come home early and I express surprise, not pleasure, surprise. I'm wearing a coat, my bags are packed and my wardrobes are clear. I'm holding a "Dear John" letter in my hand addressed to you. I tell you I'm leaving. At this point many would have asked, why? Why is it you're leaving me?

Peter continues to be drawn to the stain. Jill smashes another cup in another direction. Peter's not sure where to look

I'm leaving you, Peter, because I can't stand this any more. I want my life back; my job, my friends. I haven't seen my family in two and a half years. They have no idea what it is they did wrong and I haven't been able to tell them. We're ... We're not an us, anymore, we're a you and an I. I'm going. Tonight. For ever.

A silence. Jill stares at Peter. He finally tears his gaze away from the stains on the carpet

Peter I don't accept that.
Jill What?
Peter What you just said. I don't accept it. Any of it.

Peter heads into the kitchen

Jill It doesn't make a difference if you ——

Peter's already gone. Jill waits

Peter comes back out with a damp cloth and begins cleaning up the mess

— accept it or not. I'm leaving. Lift's coming in ten minutes.
Peter No, it's not.
Jill Oh no, it is.
Peter A1's jam packed. Lights are out, burst water main or something —
Jill Then I'll walk.
Peter In your condition?

Jill is about to say something, but can't. She strokes her stomach almost without realizing she's doing it. Peter gets up from cleaning the mess. A pause

Jill I'll make some more.
Peter I've got wine.
Jill Just for me then.

Peter hands Jill the damp cloth

Jill goes into the kitchen

Peter tidies

Peter You can use a fresh teabag.

Jill emerges from the kitchen with a cup. She sits on the sofa, takes a sip and then makes a face

Peter It's those caffeine-free bags. Said they didn't taste the same. (*He sits*)
Jill You did.
Peter And they don't, do they?

Jill says nothing

  Do they?
Jill They don't.
Peter They don't.

A silence. Jill sips her tea

Peter I'll open a bottle. (*He stands*) Red or white? Said you could
  have one glass.

Jill stares at Peter in disbelief

  You don't like the tea.

Jill continues to stare

  Be a surprise.

  Peter goes into the kitchen to get the bottle opener

*Jill tries to get her head round what's going on. Her back hurts.
Eventually she stands, walks to the door and bends to pick up the
suitcases*

  *Peter comes back in with the white and two glasses. He holds it aloft
  proudly*

Peter Went with the white. Lighter. What are you doing?
Jill This is too hard, so I thought I'd just ——
Peter I've opened the white ——
Jill — wait in the hall.

Peter sits down, opens and pours the wine into both glasses

Peter Know you said you wouldn't, but you can change your mind.

A beat

   Woman's prerogative.

A beat

   Sit back down.
Jill I'm not changing my mind.
Peter In case you might.
Jill I'm not.
Peter In case you might.

Jill puts the bags down and moves over to the sofa

Jill I've just had tea.
Peter Leave it five minutes.
Jill Who has wine straight after tea?
Peter Taste will go.
Jill Not straight after tea.
Peter Leave it five minutes.

A beat

Jill Maybe a whisky.
Peter You can't have a whisky in your condition.
Jill I could have a whisky.
Peter Whisky's very different from wine.
Jill No reason why I couldn't have a whisky.
Peter Wine is one thing. Nothing wrong with wine. One glass of wine
   in an evening, but whisky.
Jill If I wanted to have a whisky, no reason why I couldn't have a
   whisky.

Peter and Jill eyeball each other. A beat

Peter You want to have a whisky? I'll get you a whisky.

A beat

If you want to have a whisky? I'll get you a whisky. No real harm in a whisky, right? Not for you. Not for you. Have a whisky.

Peter gets up, goes over to the sideboard and pours a whisky

We'll go for the single malt. Eighteen years old. After all this is the first in what ... well, ever since we got the news. Ice?

Jill says nothing

Peter goes into the kitchen

Jill takes a deep breath and stares at the suitcases, but she can't pick them up

Peter comes back in, brandishing the glass with ice in. He thumps it down on the table. He stands, breathing heavily

You want a whisky?

A long pause

Jill (*quietly*) No.
Peter (*quietly*) No.

They both go and sit at opposite ends of the sofa. Peter moves next to Jill and places his head on her stomach. She doesn't stop him

How you getting there?
Jill Where?

Peter gestures toward the suitcases

Peter There.

Jill Getting a lift. Taxi.
Peter They'll be late.
Jill They left early. Not far to come.
Peter A1's all shot to ——
Jill They'll take another route.

A pause

Peter A1's the quickest.

Jill shrugs Peter off

Jill This is what I'm talking about.
Peter What?
Jill This. This ——
Peter Fixation.
Jill Yes.
Peter Obsessive behaviour.
Jill Obsessive behaviour. It's not healthy. It's not natural. It's driving me insane.
Peter I'll stop it then.
Jill What?
Peter I'll stop it then. Won't do it anymore.
Jill You can't just stop it.
Peter I can.
Jill You can't.
Peter I can.
Jill It's as much a part of you as ——
Peter Snapping?
Jill Snapping?
Peter Snapping.
Jill I don't snap.
Peter You do.
Jill Only when provoked.
Peter You've done it at least three times in the past ten minutes.
Jill I was being provoked.

Peter You're doing it now.
Jill I'm being provoked.

They sit in silence

Peter There.
Jill Sorry?
Peter Proved my point.
Jill I didn't say anything.
Peter My first point.
Jill About the pizza?
Peter About the fixation.

A pause. Jill stares at Peter

   Not being obsessive now.
Jill I'm going to snap.
Peter Right.
Jill FUCK.

Another silence

Peter We're making headway.

Jill doesn't respond. She sips her tea and grimaces again. It doesn't taste any better. Peter stares at the suitcases

Peter Taking them both then?
Jill Couldn't find the others. In the attic.
Peter Loft. Attic has stairs.
Jill These were to hand.
Peter Makes sense. You shouldn't be clim ——

Jill silences him with a glare. A beat

Jill I'm going to wait outside.
Peter It's cold.

Jill This is ... awkward. (*She doesn't move*) Taxi'll be here soon.
Peter So will the pizza. Free pizza.
Jill Only if they're late.
Peter They'll be late. Not here by now, they'll be late.

Peter's proved his point. Jill has an idea

Jill There are side roads.
Peter Sorry?
Jill Side roads.
Peter No.
Jill There are always side roads. Might be longer, but better than waiting.
Peter No. Checked.
Jill Through Mill Hill?
Peter Jittery lights. In its way, just as bad.
Jill Spaniards Inn?
Peter Bottleneck. Be stacking up for miles.
Jill Past the pond ——
Peter No ——
Jill Round the back of the posh flats ——
Peter Tore them down ——

Jill starts to enjoy herself

Jill The posh ones. You're thinking of the round ones ... Yes ... Through St. Patrick's, on to Davenham. Second le —— No, first, no second left, as if you're avoiding the dodgy butcher ——
Peter One with bad breath?
Jill One with the bow legs. You do the wiggly bit, speed bumps are annoying, but you come out at the end of the A1. Five minutes away.

A beat

Peter slowly gets up from the sofa. Walks over to the sideboard, opens the drawer and takes out the "A - Z". He flicks through it, till he finds the area. He studies it very carefully

Peter Go left to avoid the butcher, and the road's one-way. Can't go
     left to avoid the butcher, the road's one-way. Got to take second left,
     which takes ——
Jill That's what I said, second left.
Peter I'm saying you have to take second left.
Jill You have to take second left.
Peter That's what I'm saying.
Jill That's what I'm saying.

Peter looks at the map again

Peter Will he know that?
Jill Chances are.
Peter They left late.
Jill Even so.
Peter I think we'll make it.
Jill Find out soon.
Peter We will.
Jill We will.

*Both go and sit on the sofa and wait in an effort to prove the other one
wrong. They wait. Eventually ...*

     What will you do?
Peter I'm confident.

A beat

Jill About this?
Peter About ...

Jill gesticulates wildly at the suitcases, her coat ...

Jill ...This.
Peter Woo you.

Jill doesn't react

Woo you.

Jill Woo me?

Peter Like I once did.

Jill When did you ever woo me?

Peter At the start.

Jill That was wooing?

Peter That was wooing.

Jill That was wooing.

Peter I'll do the same again.

Jill You know I've ——

Peter Changed. Yes ——

Jill Made up my mind ——

Peter Yes, no ——

Jill Yes ——

Peter I don't accept that ——

Jill You can't ——

Peter I have ——

Jill But you can't. You can't not accept it. When I stand up and leave, am no longer in this flat. No longer occupy the same space as you. You'll have to accept it. It will be.

Peter considers this

Peter Unless ——

Jill There's no unless. How can there possibly be an unless?

Peter Unless everyone else decides to use the side roads, thus rendering them as jam-packed and useless as the rest of the A1, in which case he'll be lucky if he gets here in forty-five minutes.

A pause

Jill You can't let it go, can you?

Peter It occurred to me.

Jill You shouldn't have even been thinking about it.

Peter It's on my mind.

Jill It shouldn't be on your mind. I should be on your ... I'm getting a biscuit.

Jill heads into the kitchen

Peter Another one?
Jill (*off*) All things considered.

Peter has an idea. He goes into the bedroom

Jill comes out of the kitchen with a handful of biscuits

Jill So we agree then?
Peter (*off*) What?
Jill We agree then.
Peter (*off*) We agree.
Jill That I'm leaving you.
Peter (*off*) What?
Jill That I'm leaving you.

Peter comes back in, wearing his coat and holding a rucksack with clothes stuffed into it

Peter That one of us is leaving, yes.
Jill I'm leaving you.
Peter Perhaps.
Jill I've packed my suitcases. Both of them.
Peter Yes.
Jill They're there. By the door.
Peter I see them.
Jill Which means, I'm the one who's leaving. Me. I'm leaving you.
    Me. Me leaving you. Me.

A beat

Peter If I walk out first, I'll be the one leaving you.
Jill Why would you walk out first?
Peter If I decided.
Jill Have you?
Peter Have I?

Jill Have you decided to walk out first?
Peter I'm deciding.

A pause. They stare at each other

   Yes. I'm leaving.
Jill You don't have a suitcase.
Peter I've adapted.

Jill thinks

Jill Pizza'll be here soon.
Peter I'll meet them in the hallway. Have some now, leave the rest for
   later. Provisions.

Jill's running out of ideas

Jill You can't.
Peter Do you want me to stay?
Jill Yes.

*Peter considers this. Peter puts down his rucksack, takes his coat off
and sits back on the sofa*

Peter Knew we'd sort things out. I was thinking about names.
Jill Nothing's sorted.

*A beat. Peter gets off the sofa, puts his coat on and picks up the rucksack.
A pause*

Jill You're walking out on me?
Peter See how you enjoy it.
Jill You're walking out on me to prove that me walking out on you is
   not a nice thing to do?

A pause

Peter Partly.

A pause

Jill Partly or completely?

A pause

Peter Completely.
Jill You don't really want to leave, do you?
Peter Not really. No.

Peter puts down his rucksack, takes his coat off and sits back on the sofa. Jill goes and sits next to him

Jill Better?
Peter You've still got your coat on.
Jill I'm still leaving.
Peter Oh.

They sit in silence

Jill What's on it?

A pause

Peter Usual.
Jill Which usual?
Peter Which usual?
Jill Weekday usual or weekend usual?
Peter What day is it?
Jill Tuesday.

Peter doesn't need to reply. A pause

   Good. Deep pan's too much ——
Peter During the week.

Jill During the week.
Peter Weekend's a different kettle of fish.
Jill Naturally.

They continue to wait

   You'll ...

A pause

   ... You'll be all right.
Peter Possibly.
Jill No question. Just go back to the way you were. Before you and
   I ... before we decided to ... start afresh. New beginning. That's
   important.
Peter It is.
Jill Of course.
Peter Yes.
Jill Do all the things you ——
Peter Were never allowed to do ——
Jill — never had a chance to do ... What weren't you allowed to do?
Peter There were things.
Jill Like what?
Peter Lots of them.

A pause. Jill waits for an answer

Jill There weren't any.
Peter Potholing.
Jill Potholing?
Peter In all the years we've been married, I've never potholed.
Jill Why do you want to go potholing?
Peter Why have you never let me go potholing?
Jill You can go potholing if you want to.
Peter I can now.

A pause

Jill stands and goes to the door

Jill I'm going to wait outsi ——
Peter Needlework.
Jill You're just making them up now.
Peter Horse riding.
Jill They terrify you.
Peter I'll overcome my fears.
Jill You cancelled my lessons, because you didn't like animals bigger
    than yourself.
Peter The experience has made me stronger.
Jill Great.
Peter It is.
Jill I'm going. (*She moves to the suitcase*)
Peter (*quickly*) It's not your decision to make.

A beat

Jill It's my body. It's my life that's ... stopped. I'm the one stays in. I'm
    the one doesn't work, doesn't see family, doesn't see friends ... Not
    my decision to ——
Peter We decided it was best. Considering. I'm no different.
Jill You work.
Peter Need to. Don't like it. Rather stay here and watch you ——
Jill Watch me what? Watch me get bigger? Watch it kick? It isn't
    going to ——

*Peter jumps up from the sofa. He sings "Wuthering Heights" by Kate
Bush*

    Why won't you accept this?

*Peter continues to sing "Wuthering Heights". Jill marches to the door,
opens it and picks up the suitcases*

*Peter moves quickly and slams the door shut with an extremely loud
bang*

I'm going. Move away from the door.
Peter It's not your decision to make. It's both of ours.
Jill I have to be where things are real again. None of this is re ——

Peter grabs Jill and shakes her hard. She drops the suitcases

Peter It's whatever we say it is. In here it's whatever we say it is. We're a
team. There's no one else. After all we've been through, you and me ...
and it. No one else. We are an us. All three are an us. No one else.
Jill No.
Peter No one else. Us three.
Jill But it's not ——

Peter pulls her tightly towards him, stopping the words with the hug

But out there it's ——
Peter So stay in here.

Jill resists

Stay in here. (*He hugs Jill*)

Jill lets herself be hugged

Jill I want ——
Peter Yes.
Jill I want it so badly.
Peter Then have it. You've got it. Nothing needs to change.

*A beat. The intercom buzzes. Peter and Jill stare at the intercom. Peter
looks at his watch. The intercom buzzes again. No one moves*

Taxi?

*Jill shakes her head. The intercom buzzes. Peter looks at his watch
again. He answers the intercom*

Peter (*into the intercom*) Hello?
Voice (*off*) Pizza.

Peter doesn't answer. A slow smile spreads across his face

Hello?
Peter (*into the intercom; smugly*) You're late.
Voice (*off*) By like a minute.
Peter (*into the intercom*) Late is late. I'll just get the lift. Won't be a moment.

Peter smiles. Jill smiles back. He strokes her stomach. She puts her hand on his

Peter exits

Jill is left on her own. She looks at her stomach

Jill I want you so badly.

Jill carefully removes her coat and places it over the back of the sofa. She slowly unbuttons and removes her shirt. She wears a makeshift harness holding several cushions over her stomach. The harness shouldn't look new, but rather something that has been put together quickly, then crafted at a later date. Painfully as if it's a physical part of her, she lifts the harness over her head. It's an effort. She holds it gently and tenderly lowers it on to the sofa so the cushions are sitting, propped against the arm. She thinks about touching it, but they're just cushions. She runs her hand over her newly flat stomach

Jill places her coat and shirt over one arm, picks up the suitcases and walks out the flat in her bra. At no point does she look back

The stage is empty. A lift tings and we hear the doors open

Peter comes back into the flat. He carries several large pizza boxes and balances a big bottle of Coke under his arm

Peter You should have seen his face. Didn't like handing it over, not one bit. Probably comes out his wages. Still, law of the jungle. (*He places the boxes on the coffee table. He sees the cushions propped up against the arm*) Oh.

Peter sinks on to the sofa, unable to take his eyes off the cushions. He reaches out and strokes them tenderly. A pause. He opens up the top pizza box and takes out a slice

(*To the cushions*) I got you pineapple.

Peter sits on the sofa next to the pile of cushions and eats the pizza mechanically with no emotion

The Lights fade

THE END

FURNITURE AND PROPERTY LIST

On stage: Sofa
Coffee table
Units. *On them*: photos showing Peter and Jill in various
    locations around Britain
Sideboard with drawer. *On it*: Bottle of whisky; glasses
    In drawer: A - Z
Pouffe with storage space inside. *In it*: video manual
Pictures on wall
Clocks
Television
Video
Thermostat
Telephone
Intercom
Two suitcases

Off stage: Keys, briefcase, two bottles of white wine, one of red (**Peter**)
Knife (**Peter**)
Handbag containing brown paper bag, letter (**Jill**)
Glass of water (**Peter**)
Bourbon biscuit, digestive biscuit (**Peter**)
Two cups of tea (**Jill**)
Damp cloth (**Peter**)
Cup of tea (**Jill**)
Two glasses (**Peter**)
Ice (in glass) (**Peter**)
Handful of biscuits (**Jill**)
Rucksack with clothes stuffed into it (**Peter**)
Several large pizza boxes, big bottle of Coke (**Peter**)

Personal: **Peter**: watch
Jill: makeshift harness stuffed with cushions to look
    like a baby bump

LIGHTING PLOT

Practical fittings required: nil

To open: General interior lighting

Cue 1   **Peter** eats the pizza mechanically with no emotion   (Page 27)
             Lights fade

EFFECTS PLOT

9 780573 121982